UNDERSTANDING
OBESITY

UPFRONT HEALTH

Published in the United States of America by Cherry Lake Publishing
Ann Arbor, Michigan
www.cherrylakepublishing.com

Reading Adviser: Marla Conn MS, Ed., Literacy specialist, Read-Ability, Inc.

Photo Credits: ©EyeEm/Getty Images, cover, ©Digital Vision/Getty Images, 1, ©Michael Greenberg/Getty Images, 5, ©SolStock/Getty Images, 9, ©Jose Luis Pelaez Inc/Getty Images, 10, ©Fertnig/Getty Images, 15, ©iStockphoto/Getty Images, 19, ©Thomas Barwick/Getty Images, 20, ©Johner RF/Getty Images, 23, ©iStockphoto/Getty Images, 25, ©wundervisuals/Getty Images, 27, ©UntitledImages/Getty Images, 29, ©iStockphoto/Getty Images, 30

Copyright ©2020 by Cherry Lake Publishing
All rights reserved. No part of this book may be reproduced or utilized in any form or by any means without written permission from the publisher.

Library of Congress Cataloging-in-Publication Data has been filed and is available at catalog.loc.gov

Cherry Lake Publishing would like to acknowledge the work of The Partnership for 21st Century Learning.
Please visit www.p21.org for more information.

Printed in the United States of America
Corporate Graphics

ABOUT THE AUTHOR

Matt Chandler is the author of more than 35 non-fiction children's books. He lives in New York with his wife Amber and his children Zoey and Oliver. When he isn't busy researching or writing his next book, Matt travels the country bringing his school author visits and writing workshops to elementary and middle school students.

TABLE OF CONTENTS

CHAPTER 1

The World of Obesity

Two billion people worldwide are overweight. Of those, 650 million are obese. What is the difference between being overweight and obese? Doctors use a formula called Body **Mass** Index (BMI) to measure healthy weight. BMI divides a person's weight by their height squared. A person with a BMI of 25 or more is overweight. A person with a BMI of 30 or higher is considered obese.

The **CDC** classifies obesity as a national **epidemic** in the United States. More than 93 million adults in the United States are classified as obese. The numbers are a bit better in Canada, although one report says more than 25 percent of Canadians are obese.

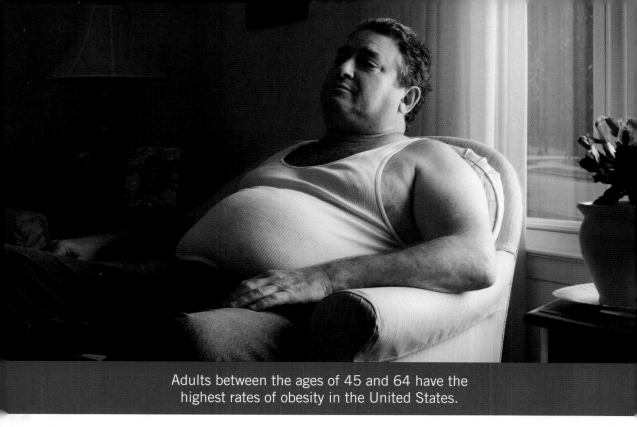

Adults between the ages of 45 and 64 have the highest rates of obesity in the United States.

The issue of obesity changes dramatically as you travel the globe. The United States has the third-largest population in the world, with about 325 million people. The obesity rate is more than 38 percent. But across the ocean, the numbers get much better. China has the largest population on Earth, well over one billion people. Yet only seven percent of the population is classified as obese. India has the second-largest population in the world, also over one billion citizens. Yet India has the lowest rate of obesity in the world, at just five percent.

The Science behind How Your Body Burns Calories

Counting calories is something many people do to help themselves stay healthy. But how does your body burn a calorie?

First, what is a calorie? A calorie is a unit of energy. Scientifically, a calorie is the amount of heat it takes to raise the temperature of one gram of water one degree. Your body needs energy to function—to walk, run, and work. You are even burning calories reading this book. When you eat, your body converts half of the nutrients in the food to energy you can use. When you burn more calories than you consume, you lose weight.

Why is there such a difference in obesity rates in different countries? There are a few factors that influence this. In India, almost 200 million people are **undernourished**. They do not have enough to eat. In China, citizens walk more steps daily than almost any country in the world. They also eat a diet heavy in fish and vegetables. Compare that to America, where there are roughly 910 cars per 1,000 people and fast-food consumption is the norm. Now you can start to see why obesity rates vary so much between the countries.

Lack of exercise and poor diets are the two leading causes of obesity. The impact obesity has on people's lives can be devastating.

Global Obesity

We have discussed the rate of obesity in the world's largest countries. But what about the rest of the world? Is obesity a global epidemic? The answer is, obesity is different in every country. In parts of Africa, famine and droughts leave millions of people without enough to eat. In many European countries, walking or biking to work is common. This leads to lower obesity rates. Search on the internet for the world's highest rates of obesity. Do you see any patterns? Are there any countries that surprise you? Why? Think about what your research tells you about global obesity.

CHAPTER 2

The Effects of Obesity

Being overweight can lead to physical, mental, and social challenges. The short-term effects of obesity are the easiest to recognize. You may find yourself out of breath from doing a normal activity like climbing a flight of stairs. As a person's weight increases, it may limit activities they can participate in. Sports can be more difficult as you gain weight. Even walking can be more difficult. This creates a problem. To lose weight, you need to exercise. But as you gain weight, exercise becomes increasingly difficult.

The short-term social impact of weight gain can be difficult to manage. People sometimes become self-conscious about their weight. Giving presentations in school or in front of colleagues may be difficult. Some people avoid social gatherings with

Gaining weight around the neck and trunk can lead to sleep-related breathing problems, making it difficult to get a good night's rest.

friends because they are ashamed of their weight. Traveling can become more challenging. Airplane seats and other public accommodations are not always accessible to obese people. People suffering from obesity often have to adjust their schedules to accommodate their weight. Even something simple like shopping for new clothes presents a challenge to someone with obesity. They may have to shop at a specialty store and pay more for their clothes than non-obese people.

Many people with type-2 diabetes have to check their blood sugar levels at home. They prick their finger and a machine tests the drop of blood.

It is the long-term effects of obesity that can be deadly. Obesity increases the risk for many diseases including:

- high blood pressure
- type-2 diabetes
- **sleep apnea**
- stroke
- heart disease
- cancer

Heart disease is the leading cause of death in the United States and Canada. There is a direct link between obesity and heart disease.

Many of these diseases occur as people get older. This is a problem because as we age, it becomes more difficult to lose weight. That is in part because the human body loses muscle as it ages and replaces it with fat. It can also become more difficult to exercise as you age, making the challenge even greater.

Apples vs. Candy Bars

Do you like candy bars? If you traded one candy bar each week for an apple, would it make a difference in a year? Let's say that your favorite candy bar has 285 calories and 15 grams of fat. That means in one year you would consume 14,820 calories and 780 grams of fat. An average apple has just 53 calories and .2 grams of fat. Over the same year that adds up to 2,756 calories and 10.4 grams of fat. One small change to your diet can save you more than 12,000 calories and 700 grams of fat!

The Cost of Obesity

Nothing is more important than your health. But there is also a huge financial cost tied to obesity. It is estimated that healthcare related to obesity costs more than $150 billion every year in the United States alone.

Then there are the costs at work. Obese employees are out sick more often. They cost more for health insurance benefits than a person in the range of healthy weight. They are also less productive on average when they are at work. Obesity in the workplace costs employers more than $73 billion annually in the United States.

Prevalence of Self-Reported Obesity Amount U.S. Adults by State, 2017

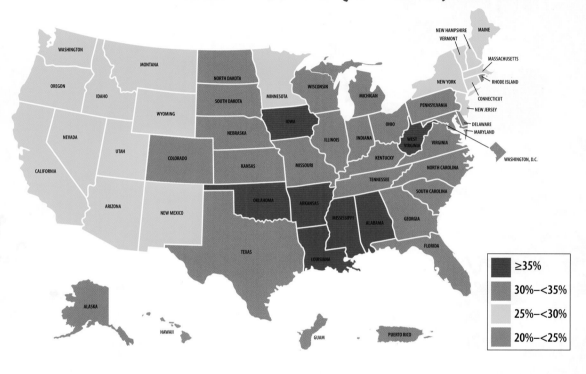

Legend:
- ≥35%
- 30%–<35%
- 25%–<30%
- 20%–<25%

Obesity Prevalence in 2017 Varies Across States and Territories
- All states had more than 20% of adults with obesity.
- 20% to less than 25% of adults had obesity in 2 states (Colorado and Hawaii) and the District of Columbia.
- 25% to less than 30% of adults had obesity in 19 states.
- 30% to less than 35% of adults had obesity in 22 states, Guam, and Puerto Rico.
- 35% or more adults had obesity in 7 states (Alabama, Arkansas, Iowa, Louisiana, Mississippi, Oklahoma, and West Virginia).
- The South (32.4%) and the Midwest (32.3%) had the highest prevalence of obesity, followed by the Northeast (27.7%), and the West (26.1%).

Source: https://www.cdc.gov/brfss/

CHAPTER 3

Obesity and Young People

According to the CDC, nearly one in five children in America are obese. So what causes childhood obesity? The short answer is most often a combination of poor diet and lack of exercise. But there can be other factors. Where you live and how much money your family has can contribute to childhood obesity. Children in low-income households may have less access to fresh fruits and vegetables. They eat more fast food and highly processed foods. Children living in high-crime areas may not have the opportunity to exercise because their parents may not feel it is safe to be outside.

About 75 percent of high school students do not get enough exercise, and almost 20 percent drink soda every day.

Genetics can also play a role in childhood obesity. Children can be born with genes from their parents that make them more at risk of being overweight. Genetic testing is available to help parents identify if their child is at risk. Then, parents can take steps to build a diet and exercise plan for their child to help overcome those genetic traits.

Even if it isn't genetic, many children with overweight parents grow up to be overweight. Parents often pass along their eating habits to their children. What they cook at home and pack for lunch may reflect their own poor eating habits.

Healthy Choices

Making healthier choices is hard. Junk food is everywhere. Bad habits are tough to break. But you can make changes. Being healthier begins with baby steps, like trading a candy bar for an apple. There are plenty of other things you can do. Find a fun way to exercise every day. It could be walking your dog or playing a game of pickup basketball with your friends. If you go to a fast-food restaurant, try something healthy on the menu. What other ways can you think of to make small changes to your daily habits to be healthier?

Being overweight or obese can also present social challenges for children. Bullying is a major concern for children who are overweight. One study found obese children are 65 percent more likely to be bullied. Students who are bullied often become more isolated. One study found that as many as 160,000 students are absent from schools in the United States on any given day because of fear of bullying.

Researchers at UCLA have also linked obesity in children to several emotional **disorders**. Doctors found obese children had higher rates of depression, learning disabilities, and **ADHD**.

That may sound scary. However, the best time to form better habits and get healthy is when you are young!

Impact of Food Journaling

Can you name everything you ate yesterday? You may have been eating in front of the television or while you were doing your homework. We don't pay attention when we eat, and that usually leads to eating more. Studies have shown that one of the best ways to be healthy is to keep a food journal. Writing down everything you eat keeps you accountable to yourself. If you find yourself writing "cake" three times in one day, you will see you need to make better choices.

CHAPTER 4

Addressing Obesity

For most people, weight gain creeps up slowly. A few pounds here and there add up. Eventually, you find yourself 25 pounds overweight and unsure what to do. Very few people will be successful losing weight alone. It takes a lot of help. Your family doctor can give advice and monitor your progress. Loved ones can help keep you on track. There are even online support groups that offer privacy.

Setting weight-loss goals is an important step in your journey. If you wake up and tell yourself you need to lose 25 pounds, you might become overwhelmed. But setting manageable goals gives you something to work toward. "I will lose three pounds this month" is a more realistic goal than "I need to lose 25 pounds right now!"

Young people should get 60 minutes of exercise, such as jogging, swimming, hiking, or dancing, each day.

"Outcome goals" target a specific outcome you desire. These types of goals are only one part of the successful goal-setting needed to lose weight. You need to decide how you are going to lose weight and set what are called "process goals." These goals outline the steps you must take to reach your outcome. For these two outcome goals, you might need several process goals. Examples of these are "I will not eat after 7 p.m." or "I will take a walk after dinner every night instead of playing video games." These process goals will keep you on track to reaching your outcome goals.

Drinking cold water helps the body burn calories.

In this example, let's look at how you might shape your goals:

Outcome Goal: Lose 25 Pounds.

Manageable Goal: Lose 3 pounds this month.

Process Goals:

- Replace your favorite drinks with water at breakfast for one week.
- Replace your favorite drinks with water at breakfast and lunch the second week.
- Replace your favorite drinks with water at all meals in the third week.

- Walk for 20 minutes every day for one week.
- Walk for 30 minutes every day for the second week.
- Walk for 45 minutes every day for the third week.

You have taken what seems like an impossible goal and broken it down into manageable stages. Losing 25 pounds might seem impossible. Losing three pounds feels manageable and it will give you momentum to continue!

Partnering for Your Health

Lifting something heavy is easier with a friend. The same is true for eating healthy or exercising. If you have someone working with you, it is easier. Walking every day can be boring. You might be tempted to quit. You are more likely to follow through if you have a friend walking with you. If you want to dive into that junk food after school, having someone checking on you can keep you honest. Experts say having a person by your side can lead to greater success in dieting and exercise. Who in your life could be your accountability partner?

Healthy Schools

Look around your school campus. Is it a place filled with healthy options? Do you have vending machines stocked with bottled water and healthy snacks? Does your school offer a walking club or intramural yoga classes? Do any of your classrooms have **standing desks**? How about a morning fitness routine? If your school has some of these options, that's great! Take advantage of them as part of your healthy lifestyle.

If your school doesn't have these options, this is your chance to make a difference. Do your research. Gather information on a healthy program you would like to see in your school. Put together a proposal and bring it to your school leadership. Be prepared to answer questions like:

- What will the cost be to the school?
- What will the main benefits be for students?
- How many students are likely to want to participate in the new idea?

[21ST CENTURY SKILLS LIBRARY]

Standing desks have been shown to burn extra calories and lower the risk of weight gain and obesity.

CHAPTER 5

Making Healthy Choices

If keeping a healthy weight is about calories and exercise, why isn't everyone their ideal weight? It comes down to personal choices. Each time you raise a bite of food to your lips you are making a choice. Each time you choose to go for a walk instead of watch television, you are making a choice.

People make poor choices for many different reasons. Have you ever felt sad and just wanted to lie on the couch and eat an entire gallon of ice cream? People use food to comfort themselves when they are sad, lonely, or angry. So how do you make better choices to protect your body and your health? Here are a few practical ideas to begin with:

Eating comfort foods releases chemicals in the brain that make people feel good. But exercise releases similar chemicals that make people feel happy and energized, as well.

Portion control: If you love potato chips, never eating them again probably won't work. Instead, try taking a small amount of chips and eating them slowly. Enjoy them without overeating.

Focused eating: When you focus on your food, you enjoy it more. You also eat less. If you are distracted in a movie theater, in front of the television, or while playing video games, you can consume twice as much food and not even realize it.

High-Tech Help

People often blame technology for adding to the problem of obesity. People using phones, computers, and video games may eat more and exercise less. But what about the ways technology can help you be healthier? Remember the idea of keeping a food journal? There are many apps that act as an electronic food journal. Since most people always have their phone with them, they'll be more likely to keep up with their food log.

Other apps help you track exercise, including your daily steps. Fitbits and watches can also track **heart rate***, steps, calories burned, and other health information.*

20 minutes of fun exercise: Create the habit of daily exercise. Make it fun and build up slowly. Every step you take and every jog you go on burns calories. It also creates a healthy habit. Don't try to go to the gym for two hours your first time. Start slow and build toward your long-term health.

Exercise technology can monitor speed, time,
and distance, and provide motivation.

Obesity is a deadly epidemic. In the short term, you will feel bad and live a less happy life. In the long term, it greatly increases the chances of an early death. You control your future. You get to write your own story. Make it one with a happy ending. Make good choices. Surround yourself with a support system of family and friends. And live your best life starting now!

Slow and Steady

Weight loss is a slow process. Fad diets can be dangerous and usually result in gaining weight. Research shows people who lose 1 to 2 pounds (0.5 to 1 kilogram) per week are more likely to keep the weight off.

The same is true for exercise. Start slow and steady. In the beginning, you are trying to establish good habits.

What is one thing you could do to change your diet? What is one step you could take to exercise more? Write both things down. Can you do them tomorrow? Before you know it, you will have new healthy habits!

Walking improves balance, coordination, and mood,
as well as helps to maintain a healthy weight.

Think About It

To help with obesity and weight issues, government and health groups make recommendations for exercise. The World Health Organization (WHO) suggests those ages 5 to 17 do physical activity 60 minutes a day. Most should be aerobic exercise. WHO also recommends strength-building exercise at least three times a week.

Using the library or the internet, research the difference between aerobic and strength-building exercise. What are examples of each? What happens differently in the body? Which is best for losing fat? Which is best for building muscle? Which type of exercise do you think is most important for kids? Do you agree with WHO's recommendations?

Learn More

BOOKS

Bankston, John. *Exercising Better.* Hallandale, FL: Mitchell Lane Publishers, 2018.

Claybourne, Anna. *Food and Eating.* London: Franklin Watts, 2019.

Dickmann, Nancy. *What You Need to Know about Obesity.* North Mankato, MN: Capstone Press, 2016.

Marsico, Katie. *Eat a Balanced Diet!* Ann Arbor, MI: Cherry Lake Publishing, 2015.

ON THE WEB

CDC Childhood Overweight and Obesity
https://www.cdc.gov/obesity/childhood/index.html

Fuel Up to Play 60
https://www.fueluptoplay60.com

KidsHealth
https://kidshealth.org/en/kids/center/fitness-nutrition-center.html

MyPlate Games
https://www.choosemyplate.gov/games

GLOSSARY

ADHD (AYE-dee-h-dee) a mental health issue that makes a person have trouble paying attention or sitting still; stands for attention deficit hyperactivity disorder

CDC (see-DEE-see) a U.S. government agency in charge of overseeing public health; stands for the Centers for Disease Control and Prevention

disorder (dis-OR-dur) a mental or physical illness

epidemic (ep-i-DEM-ik) a health crisis that affects many people at once

genetics (jen-ET-iks) the process of passing down qualities and characteristics, such as physical appearance and risk for disease, from parents to children

heart rate (HART REYT) the number of times the heart beats in one minute; heart rate increases when exercising

mass (MASS) the amount of physical material inside something; unlike weight, mass is not affected by gravity and is a more scientific measure than weight

sleep apnea (SLEEP AP-nee-uh) a health issue that causes a person to stop breathing for several seconds at a time while sleeping, often hundreds of times each night

standing desk (STAN-ding DESK) a tall desk designed to work without a chair

undernourished (uhn-der-NUR-isht) not having enough food or a balanced diet to grow at a normal and healthy rate

INDEX